soldier

of the

American

Revolution

—∿∿✹〰〰—

Denis Hambucken

Bill Payson

Text, photographs, and illustrations © 2011 by Denis Hambucken
Historic consulting by Bill Payson
All rights reserved.

No part of this book may be reproduced in any form or by any electronic or mechanical means including information storage and retrieval systems without permission in writing from the publisher, except by a reviewer, who may quote brief passages.

Book design and composition by Denis Hambucken
Editing by Lisa Sacks
Proofreading by Gail Cohen
Historic typefaces by Scriptorium Fonts and Walden Fonts

Library of Congress Cataloging-in-Publication Data have been applied for.
Soldier of the American Revolution
978-0-88150-958-8

Published by The Countryman Press, P.O. Box 748, Woodstock, VT 05091
Distributed by W. W. Norton & Company, Inc., 500 Fifth Avenue, New York, NY 10110

Printed in the United States of America
10 9 8 7 6 5 4 3 2 1

Acknowledgments

Many thanks to the individuals and organizations that have shared their time, knowledge, and passion with us. This book could not have been constructed without their help.

Kermit Hummel
1st New Hampshire Regiment
Todd Boothroyd, Christopher Woolf, and the 4th Regiment of Foot
Paul O'Shaughnessy, Lincoln Clark, and the 10th Regiment of Foot
Graeme Marsden and the 1st Foot Guards
Lou Sideris and the Minute Man National Historical Park
Nathan Gams

Special thanks to Eames's Rangers

Contents

Prelude to the American Revolution ——————— 6

    Intolerable Acts ————————————— 7

    Lexington and Concord ————————— 8

    Events Chronology ———————————— 10

The Colonial Militia ————————————— 12

The Soldier's Dress & Equipment ——————— 16

    Paper Cartridges ————————————— 32

    Firing the Flintlock Musket ————————— 34

    The Soldier's Ration ———————————— 43

    Literacy ———————————————— 45

    Striking Fire with Flint and Steel —————— 48

British Regulars ——————————————— 54

    The British Soldier's Dress & Equipment ——— 58

Epilogue —————————————————— 60

Index ——————————————————— 62

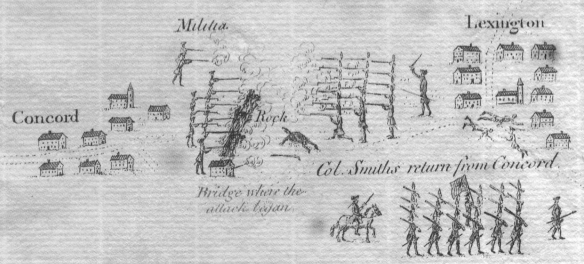

Detail of a map of the Battle of Lexington and Concord by J. De Costa published in London in 1775.

Prelude to the American Revolution

By the end of the 18th century, a rift had developed between England and its thirteen American colonies. A growing portion of the population, including immigrants from Ireland, Scotland, continental Europe, and African slaves had no direct cultural ties with England. England failed to recognize America as a maturing society and persisted in the mercantilist view that colonies were subservient territories, existing solely for the benefit of the homeland. Trade regulations were deliberately skewed to take advantage of America's natural resources while preventing colonists from competing with English merchants and manufacturers. The rivalry between France and England to control North America culminated in the French and Indian War, which started in 1754 and continued until 1763. An English victory drove the French from the continent and dragged both nations deeply into debt. The English parliament was irritated by what it saw as the colonies' inadequate financial support for a war from which they emerged safer and more prosperous. England sought to levy new taxes to rebuild its treasury and to finance its North American military presence.

Intolerable Acts

In 1765, the British Parliament enacted the Stamp Act requiring American colonists to purchase and apply stamps to documents including legal papers, newspapers, and even playing cards. Although similar taxes were levied in England, they were immediately and violently contested by Americans to the cry of "taxation without representation." The Townshend Act, an alternative tax on imported glass, lead, paint, and paper, proved equally unpopular. To protest a tax on tea, a group of dissidents calling themselves Sons of Liberty staged the Boston Tea Party by boarding a British ship and dumping its tea cargo into Boston harbor. In response, an outraged Parliament passed a series of punitive laws that became known in America as the Intolerable Acts. Among other things, these laws placed the government of Massachusetts under more direct British control and closed Boston Harbor until reparation for the lost tea was to be paid. British troops were redeployed from their frontier outposts to coastal cities to enforce the unpopular laws and tariffs. The growing presence of the "lobster backs" further fueled resentment and led to incidents including the Boston Massacre, when, fearing for their lives, British soldiers opened fire on a mob of protesters.

The BLOODY MASSACRE perpetrated in King—t—Street BOSTON on March 5ᵗʰ 1770 by a party of the 29ᵗʰ REGᵗ

Engrav'd Printed & Sold by PAUL REVERE BOSTON

Insurgents succeeded in rallying public opinion with inflammatory material such as this clearly biased depiction of the Boston Massacre engraved by Paul Revere, based on a drawing by Henry Pelham.

Lexington and Concord

In April of 1775, weary of mounting hostility, British troops under Lieutenant Colonel Francis Smith set out to seize the militia's stocks of weapons and ammunition in Concord, a town about 18 miles west of Boston. However, word of the mission had been leaked to the Sons of Liberty.

Paul Revere and William Dawes were dispatched on horseback to warn Concord and nearby towns. This odyssey was made famous as "Paul Revere's Ride" by poet Henry Wadsworth Longfellow. As they made their way through the countryside, the British troops could hear distant alarm guns spreading news of their advance. Thus realizing that he had lost the element of surprise, Colonel Smith sent a messenger back to Boston requesting reinforcements. This wise decision most probably saved his detachment from complete annihilation the following day. The first confrontation took place in Lexington, where the British troops came upon a muster of local militiamen. In the very tense and confused moments that followed, a shot was fired, setting off the first skirmish of the war. The origin of the first shot is unknown since, according to later testimonies, it is clear that both sides wanted to avoid a firefight. The militia, outnumbered by almost ten to one, was overrun quickly and suffered heavy losses. The British troops reached Concord, but they searched in vain for the arsenal that had been dispersed by the militia. During the march back to Boston, the British were continuously harassed by militiamen, now numbering several thousand. Exhausted and running out of ammunition, they were rescued by reinforcements under Brigadier General Hugh Percy. The Americans pursued the retreating British all the way to Charlestown, just east of Boston. News of the bloodshed spread quickly and rallied scores of militiamen throughout New England. Within the next few days, more than fifteen thousand armed men blockaded Boston. The siege, which was to last almost a year, marked the beginning of the American War of Independence.

The Hartwell Tavern at the Minute Man National Historical Park has been restored to look much as it did in 1775 as British troops marched by. Photo courtesy of the Minute Man National Historical Park.

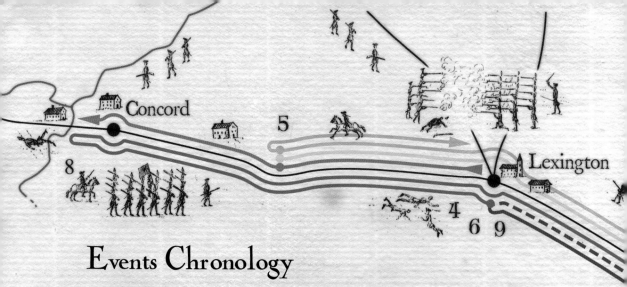

Events Chronology

1. On the night of April 18, about seven hundred British Regulars under Col. Francis Smith set out across the Charles River on a mission to seize and destroy reserves of weapons and gunpowder in Concord.

2. That same night, Paul Revere and William Dawes are dispatched to Lexington to alert John Hancock and Samuel Adams. Revere crosses the Charles River and heads north through Charlestown and Medford, while Dawes takes the overland route through Roxbury, Brookline, and Cambridge.

3. Col. Smith, realizing that he has lost the element of surprise, sends a messenger back to Boston to request reinforcements.

4. Paul Revere reaches Lexington around midnight, followed about a half hour later by William Dawes. After hypothesizing with John Hancock, Samuel Adams, and Dr. Samuel Prescott as to Smith's intentions, they decide to ride on to Concord. Prescott accompanies them.

5. Revere, Dawes, and Prescott are arrested by British troops. Dawes and Prescott escape. Dawes returns to Lexington while Prescott rides on to Concord and beyond.

6. On the morning of April 19, Col. Smith reaches Lexington and encounters a muster of about eighty militiamen. The first shots of the war are fired. The militia is quickly overrun, and Smith continues toward Concord.

7. That same morning, about one thousand men under Brigadier General Hugh Percy leave Boston on a mission to reinforce Smith's detachment.

8. Smith reaches Concord, but fails to find the weapons and gunpowder that have been dispersed and hidden. Facing mounting casualties and increasing resistance, he heads back toward Lexington.

9. Percy's detachment reaches Smith and his exhausted troops. Percy takes command of the combined forces and retreats toward Boston.

10. Fighting grows fiercer as fresh militiamen pour in from surrounding towns and organize themselves along the road ahead of the retreating column. By sundown, the British forces reach the safety of Charlestown. The siege of Boston begins.

Battle of Lexington and Concord

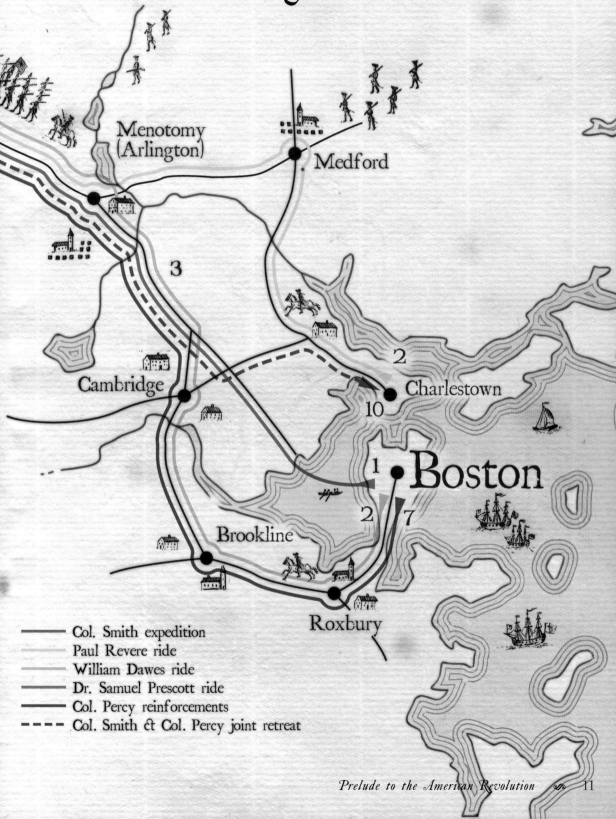

Menotomy
(Arlington)

Medford

3

Cambridge

2

Charlestown

10

1 · **Boston**

2

2   7

Brookline

Roxbury

——— Col. Smith expedition
——— Paul Revere ride
——— William Dawes ride
——— Dr. Samuel Prescott ride
——— Col. Percy reinforcements
----- Col. Smith & Col. Percy joint retreat

The Colonial Militia

The Colonial Militia

From the time of the earliest settlements, colonists had to provide for their own defense against hostile indigenous peoples and rival European nations. Militias are reserves of civilian men armed, trained, and ready to mobilize in case of danger. All able-bodied adult males, with few exceptions, were to participate in training exercises as required by town ordinances. Upon enlistment, conscripts usually signed a covenant outlining a code of conduct, duties, and rights. Since few towns had enough resources to provide their militias with any sort of equipment, it was usually expected that each man avail himself of a good firelock and prescribed quantities of gunpowder and lead.

Social classes were clearly defined in colonial America. Aside from slaves, who were excluded from service, subsistence farmers and laborers represented the lowest and most numerous class. Consequently, they also constituted the bulk of the militia. The remainder was made up of craftsmen, artisans, shopkeepers, gentlemen farmers, and other members of the middle class. Clergymen, doctors, jurists, and other officials whose role was deemed critical to the welfare of the community were usually exempt, and the very wealthy could avoid conscription by hiring stand-ins.

Militiamen, sporting an array of civilian clothes, muskets, and hunting rifles, mustered several times a year at the village green, tavern, or other landmark. Muster day was always an important event in small towns, where entertainment in any form was a rare treat. Knowing they would be scrutinized by the better part of their community, the men put forth their best effort and appearance. After the roll call, they engaged in a series of drills and marching exercises, practiced volley fire and honed their loading speed and aim. As tensions with the British establishment started to mount in the years leading to the Revolution, militias were mustered more frequently and officers with loyalist leanings were forced out.

The effectiveness and readiness of the militias depended on the fitness of the conscripts and the professionalism and zeal of the officers, who were generally elected by their own troops. Officers often drew on some military experience, many having served in the French and Indian War. On paper, the militias were outclassed by the better trained, better equipped British Army. They possessed, however, a few significant advantages. The word aim was not part of the British army's vernacular In the tradition of European warfare, large battalions faced off on open terrain, needing only to point their muskets in the direction of enemy formations to achieve effective fire. Americans were superior marksmen, being accustomed to firearms and hunting from childhood. From a long history of conflicts with Native Americans, they had learned to adopt a more modern style of guerrilla warfare. Americans fought best in wooded terrain where they could engage in fighting retreats and make the most of the familiar ground to find cover and take careful aim.

Mobilizing militias quickly over vast distances in a widely agricultural society was difficult. An elaborate network of bells, alarm guns, and messenger riders was put in place to call militiamen to arms and to spread the alarm from town to town. In some communities, a portion of the militia was designated as rapid responders, men who vowed to be ready to fight at a minute's notice. These "minutemen" were selected from the younger militiamen for their vitality and marksmanship. They trained more frequently than other militiamen and were usually equipped with military-grade muskets and bayonets that they were to keep within reach at all times. The Minutemen's quick response to the British advance toward Lexington was a key factor in the events that led to the outbreak of the war.

The Soldier's
Dress & Equipment

The Soldier's Dress & Equipment

At the very beginning of the war, what would soon be known as the Continental Army was almost entirely made of New England militiamen, few of whom were provided with any sort of equipment or uniform. Consequently, the army was a hodgepodge of colors and styles representing every level of society. Some men wore laborers' smocks and broad hats, as though they had just come from the fields, while others sported fashionable English finery or hunting frocks, but as a matter of pride, the majority put forth their best appearance.

The weaponry was as diverse as the men. There were a few rifles, but most men carried smoothbore muskets, supplemented with a bayonet, a tomahawk, or a sword.

1. Beaver felt hat
2. Knapsack
3. Canteen
4. Bayonet scabbard
5. Longstockings
6. Powder horn
7. Cartridge box
8. Flintlock musket
9. Bayonet
10. Coat
11. Waistcoat
12. Breeches

Waistcoat and Coat

A self-respecting man would not be seen in formal settings without a waistcoat and coat. The waistcoat, a form-fitting sleeveless jacket, evolved into the vest that still endures today. The large number of buttons harks back to earlier times when it was an indicator of wealth. In the 18th century, buttons were worn by everyone, but they were still valuable enough to be saved from old garments and used over and over again.

The buttons below are made of brass, horn, and pewter.

Neckerchief

All men wore some sort of neck cloth, ranging from the upscale cravat adorned with ruffles or lace to the working-class neckerchief, a square of lightweight linen or cotton wrapped around the neck and loosely tied in front with a simple knot.

Shirt

The shirt was an undergarment seldom worn without a waistcoat or jacket. Unlike other articles of clothing that were form-fitting, it was of a simple and generous cut. The shirt was mid-thigh, or even knee-length to serve as a nightshirt, and it served as underwear when tucked into breeches.

Cocked Hat

Men and women almost always wore hats. For men, broad-brimmed beaver felt hats were the most fashionable type. The habit of cocking hats on one, two, or three sides developed among the upper class as etiquette dictated that hats be held in hand in many formal circumstances. In an army without uniforms, colored cockades were often used to distinguish officers and functionaries.

Cap

Many men carried simple cloth or wool caps that could be stuffed in a pocket and worn indoors, or while sleeping to keep warm.

Breeches

Through the 18th century, girls and boys wore dresses until the age of five or six, when boys were "breeched," that is, fitted with their first pair of breeches. Breeches were snug to the leg and loose in the seat to allow comfortable movement and sitting.

Longstockings and Garters

Woolen or linen stockings were
worn year round by all but the most
affluent, who might switch to silk or
cotton in warm weather. Stockings
were held up by ribbons or
leather garters just below
the knee.

Buckle Shoes

Until the end of the 18th century, both shoes in a pair were usually shaped on the same straight last. This meant that before the shoes were broken in and started to conform to the wearer's feet, there was no distinction between left and right shoes. Shoe buckles were bought separately, or saved from previous shoes. They featured two sets of double prongs that hooked to straps on both sides of the shoe.

Gaiters

Gaiters were worn over the ankles; some were tall enough to reach above the knee. They were made of painted canvas or leather to keep rain, snow, gravel, and dirt out of the shoes. Similar gaiters were worn by the United States armed forces as late as the Korean War.

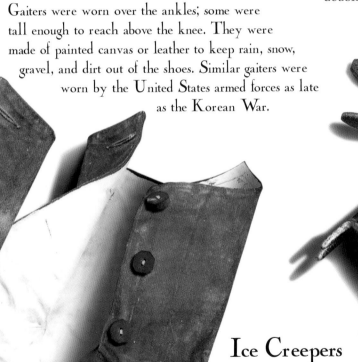

Ice Creepers

Since leather soles performed poorly on ice or packed snow, soldiers equipped themselves with sets of cleats that were fastened with leather straps over their shoes. In very cold weather, the ability to walk quickly across frozen lakes and rivers presented a significant strategic advantage.

Pick and Brush

Cleaning the flash pan between shots was important because sooty gunpowder residue could obstruct the touchhole or, owing to its hygroscopic nature, it could draw enough humidity from the air over time to spoil the following charge. The pick and brush were often tethered to the cartridge box or to a coat button.

Ramrod

Flintlock Musket

The British standard issue musket was the Tower flintlock that was eventually nicknamed "Brown Bess." It was a smoothbore muzzle-loading musket that shot a three-quarter-inch lead ball. Smoothbore muskets were less accurate than rifles, but because they fired loose-fitting balls, they were easier and faster to load. A trained soldier could fire off three or four shots per minute. Large stocks of British military muskets found their way to North America during the French and Indian War or landed in the hands of the militias as arsenals were raided at the start of the Revolution. Fowling pieces and military muskets of French, Dutch, and Spanish origins were also in use.

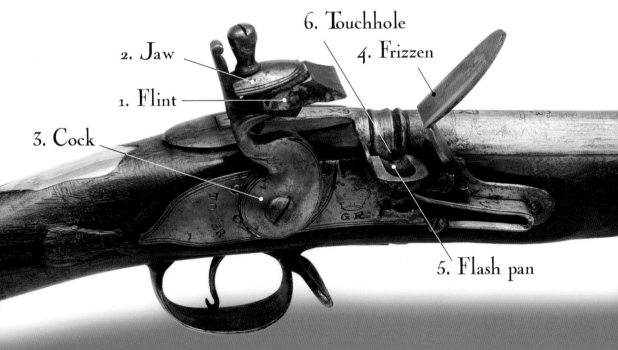

6. Touchhole

2. Jaw

4. Frizzen

1. Flint

3. Cock

5. Flash pan

The Flintlock Mechanism

A sharp flint (1) is secured in the jaws (2) of the spring-loaded cock (3). When released, the flint at once pushes the frizzen (4) open and throws sparks into the flash pan (5), where it ignites the priming gunpowder. The ignition is communicated to the charge through the touchhole (6).

Cartridge Box

To increase the rate of fire, lead balls and gunpowder were packaged into paper cartridges kept in specialized leather bags. A perforated wood block held the cartridges upright so they could quickly be retrieved by feel with a single hand. The oversized flap kept rain or snow out while space below the block accommodated various supplies and accessories. The example shown here features a small pocket for a spare flint and a tethered screwdriver for the maintenance of the musket.

Gun Flints

No factor determined the reliability of the flintlock more than the sharpness and quality of the flint. Lacking a satisfactory American source, the colonies imported gun flints by the millions from Europe. The best flint deposits occurred in regions of France and England where flintknapping had developed into a flourishing cottage industry. Small strips of leather or lead were necessary to properly seat the irregular surface of the flints into the jaws of the lock. A good flint could last dozens of shots.

Paper Cartridges

The cartridge is a simple tube of paper with a lead ball at one end and a pre-measured amount of gunpowder. The paper also served as wadding to keep the gunpowder tightly packed and to prevent the loose-fitting ball from rolling out of the barrel.

Tallow and Brick Dust

The metal parts of the musket were polished with an abrasive
paste made of tallow and brick dust. The tallow offered the added
benefit of forming a greasy protective film. Customary spit and polish
dictated that soldiers scour their muskets obsessively, sometimes to the point of
wearing them out prematurely. As the war progressed however, a growing number
of regiments took to "browning" their guns by allowing a thin layer of rust to form
on them. When oiled or waxed, the rust formed a dark brown protective coating
that rendered the gun less conspicuous in sharpshooting and skirmishing
actions and prevented glare from interfering with the soldiers' aim.

Musket Tools

Compact tools necessary for the maintenance of the musket typically included screwdriver heads of several sizes and sometimes a pick or a pushpin to remove the pins that held the musket components together.

Musket Worm & Ball Puller

Gunpowder was a very dirty propellant. Up to 50 percent of each charge remained in the barrel in the form of a sooty and somewhat corrosive residue. The barrel was cleaned with hot water, flax tow, and a musket worm. The base of the worm was threaded to the end of the ramrod, and the two corkscrew prongs were loaded with flax tow and run up and down the barrel. When a gunpowder charge was spoiled by humidity or fouling, the lead ball had to be extracted with a ball puller, which could also be threaded to the ramrod. The sharp screw was driven into the lead to grab hold of the ball.

Paper Cartridges

Prior to the use of paper cartridges, musketeers were equipped with bandoliers of apostles, rows of wooden flasks each containing pre-measured quantities of gunpowder. The advent of the paper cartridge further sped reloading by incorporating the lead ball and the paper that was used as wadding. At first, the use of cartridges was limited by the scarcity of paper, but by the American War of Independence it had been adopted by all the modern armies in the world. American militiamen were usually expected to prepare their own as needed to replenish their cartridge boxes.

1. Folding opposite corners of a rectangular piece of paper together and cutting along the fold produces two trapezoid shapes.

2. The paper is rolled around a wooden dowel of the diameter of the ball.

3. The end of the paper tube is formed around the rounded end of the dowel, and closed with a ligature.

4. The dowel is removed and a lead ball is inserted. A second ligature secures it at the bottom of the cartridge.

5. After a measured amount of gunpowder has been poured into the cartridge, the paper is folded to produce a narrow tab.

6. The tab is tucked beneath the slanted edge of one of the layers of paper.

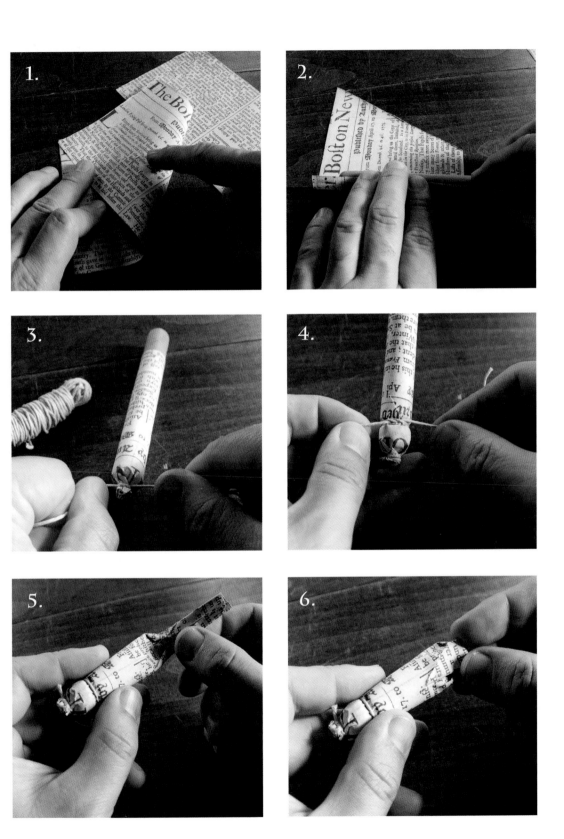

Firing the Flintlock Musket

1. The lock is half cocked to yield access to the flash pan.

2. A cartridge is retrieved from the cartridge box.

3. The cartridge is torn open with the teeth.

4. The flash pan is primed with a small amount of gunpowder.

5. The frizzen is closed over the flashpan to secure the priming charge.

6. The rest of the gunpowder is poured into the barrel.

7. The lead ball and paper are pushed into the barrel.

8. The charge is rammed into the breech and compacted with the ramrod.

9. The lock is fully cocked, and the musket is ready to be fired.

Casting Lead Balls

Since standardized calibers were not yet the norm at the militia level, men carried muskets with a wide range of bore diameters. Soldiers often had to cast their own musket balls with molds that were specific to each weapon. For this reason, militia covenants sometimes required each man to carry a certain quantity of lead, rather than a specific number of musket balls. Lead's relatively low melting temperature made it easy to cast balls with small casting ladles and scissor molds at fireplaces or campfires. Some soldiers carried reserves of lead balls in leather pouches.

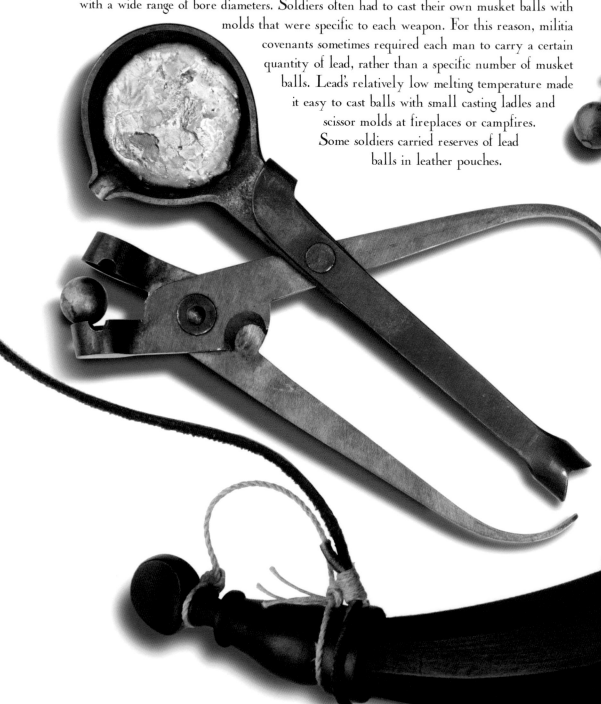

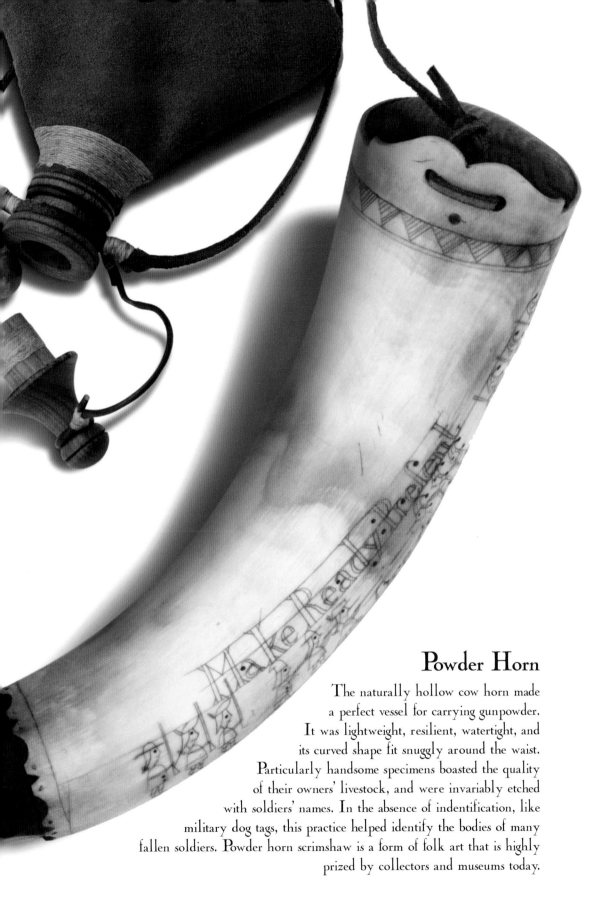

Powder Horn

The naturally hollow cow horn made
a perfect vessel for carrying gunpowder.
It was lightweight, resilient, watertight, and
its curved shape fit snuggly around the waist.
Particularly handsome specimens boasted the quality
of their owners' livestock, and were invariably etched
with soldiers' names. In the absence of indentification, like
military dog tags, this practice helped identify the bodies of many
fallen soldiers. Powder horn scrimshaw is a form of folk art that is highly
prized by collectors and museums today.

Tomahawk

Some militias were equipped with hatchets inspired by Native American tomahawks. These were extremely versatile tools used not only as throwing or hacking weapons, but also for shaping wood implements, cutting and splitting firewood, for butchering animals, and for driving nails or tent stakes.

Bayonet

Nothing struck fear in the hearts of soldiers like the sight of glistening bayonets. The bayonet is a stabbing blade that was mounted at the tip of the musket barrel during combat. The triangular cross-section provided extra rigidity and was easy to grind to a very sharp point. The bayonet became a weapon of last resort in very close combat when soldiers had no time to reload.

Canteen

Canteens were made in a variety of styles and from a range of materials that included wood, tin, leather, and gourds. Vinegar and honey or sugar were sometimes added to the water to create what was known as switchel, a mixture that was thought to make water safer, to ward off scurvy, and to protect from heatstroke.

Knapsack

Soldiers carried personal belongings and sometimes food rations in large canvas knapsacks or haversacks.

Blanket

The unprocessed wool of the 18th century was rich in lanolin that gave it superior water-shedding properties, making the blanket more effective in damp conditions. The blanket was sometimes used as a secondary bag; it was wrapped around supplies and bundled around a sling carried over the shoulder.

Sewing Kit

A sewing kit comprising a few spare buttons, thread, and needles in a needle case (this one carved out of the tip of an antler) was useful in the absence of women, who would ordinarily be expected to mend clothing. The coarse thread was used for repairing shoes, and other leather or heavy canvas goods.

Shaving

Scant hygiene in the Continental Army was a chronic problem that was largely credited for the rampant outbreaks of typhus, typhoid fever, dysentery, smallpox, and pneumonia. Dirty as they often were, soldiers in the normal course of their enlistment were expected to be clean shaven several times a week. Few men shaved themselves or even carried shaving kits, because the exercise was too perilous without a mirror. Enlisted barbers plied their trade within their regiments, or civilian barbers were employed.

Mess Kit

Soldiers had to procure their own mess kits. These usually included a wooden bowl or trencher, a tin cup, a spoon, and a knife. Until the second half of the 19th century, knives with broad blades were often used to scoop and stab food in lieu of forks and spoons.

The Soldier's Ration

On November 4, 1775, the Continental Congress passed a resolution defining the ration of the enlisted soldier:

Resolved, that a ration consist of the following kind and quantity of provisions, viz:

1 lb. of beef, or 3/4 lb. pork, or 1 lb. salt fish, per day.

1 lb. of bread or flour per day.

3 pints of peas, or beans per week, or vegetables equivalent, at one dollar per bushel for peas or beans.

1 pint of milk per man per day, or at the rate of 1/72 of a dollar.

1 half pint of rice, or 1 pint of Indian meal (cornmeal) per man per week.

1 quart of spruce beer or cider per man per day, or nine gallons of molasses per company of 100 men per week.

3 lb. candles to 100 men per week for guards.

24 lb. of soft or 8 lb. of hard soap for 100 men per week.

The colonies' prosperous farms produced an abundance of food. However, gathering and distributing it to concentrations of many thousands of men was an unprecedented challenge for the colonists. Companies might go for days or weeks without proper meals while an overabundance of meat and vegetables might be spoiling elsewhere. Options for preserving food were limited. Owing to shortages of the salt that was necessary for curing meat, cattle and pigs were sometimes marched with the troops. Some, for lack of proper forage, became so emaciated that they were hardly worth the slaughtering. Dry peas and beans were staples, but fresh fruits and vegetables were often lacking. Where bread could not be baked in sufficient quantities, soldiers were supplied with flour or with hard bread (pictured below), a type of heavy, unleavened biscuit that was baked repeatedly until brick-hard and that could be preserved almost indefinitely if kept dry.

Spectacles

Only the wealthy could afford eyeglasses; others had to make do with
whatever vision impairment might afflict them. Glasses were rarely made
to order. Shoppers picked from a limited selection of ready-made glasses
that were usually imported from Europe. Early eyeglasses were
constructed with loops through which a ribbon
was threaded, then tied behind the head.

Traveling Ink Stand

Few soldiers took the
time to write during
their service, mostly
because very few did
so in the course of
their civilian life, but
also because carrying
the necessary ink,
quills, and paper was
cumbersome and messy.
The traveling ink stand
included a small vial of ink and
a few quills inside a wood or metal
shell.

Literacy

During the Revolution, American soldiers were the most literate soldiers in the world. At the beginning of the war, the army was almost entirely recruited in New England, where approximately 80 percent of adults could read as compared to less than 40 percent in England. The unusual practice of teaching reading to boys and girls from every level of society probably found its origins in Puritanism that promoted individual Bible study. Reading and writing were taught separately, the former often without the latter. Of the people that could read printed material, only a small percentage could write and read cursive text. These were typically wealthy landowners, merchants, clerks, clergymen, or others whose occupations required correspondence or record keeping. An important part of penmanship consisted in mastering the art of carving goose or turkey quills.

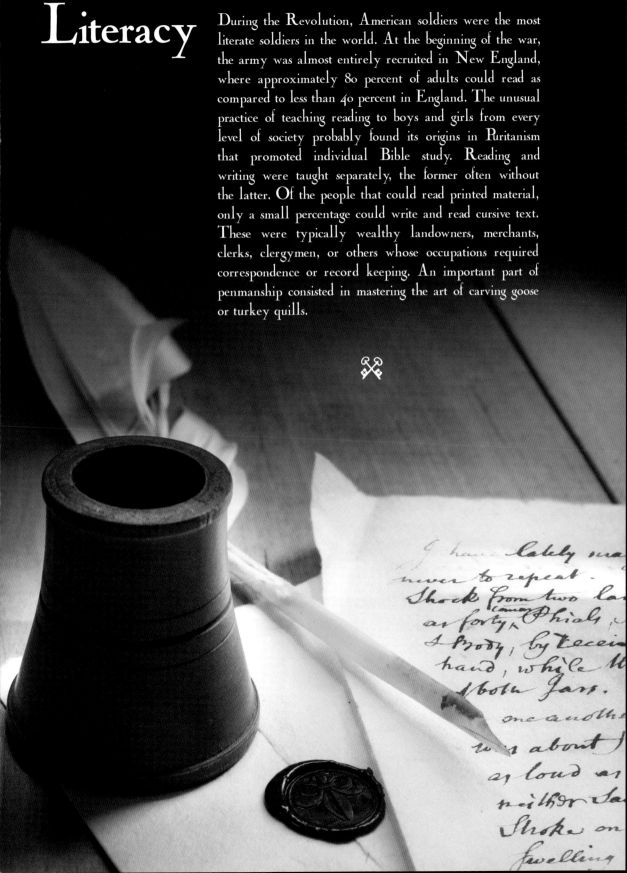

Tinder Box

Fire-starting kits were typically carried in tin boxes. When necessary, a little wax or tallow could be rubbed on the rim to render the box waterproof.

Steel Striker and Flint

A glancing strike with hardened steel on the sharp edge of a flint produces extremely hot sparks. These small fragments of steel are so overheated by the impact that they partially burn in contact with oxygen in the air.

Birch Bark & Tinder Fungus

The birch tree was particularly useful for starting fires. Its oily bark catches fire even when wet and burns vigorously. The birch tree harbors two types of tinder fungi, so named because when dry, they can be ignited with sparks and they quickly form persistent embers, much like char cloth.

Char cloth

Char cloth is made of small pieces of linen or cotton cloth carbonized over a fire in a metal box. Material from old rags works best because the frayed surface is more apt to catch sparks.

Flax Tow

As the name of the tinderbox implies, dry tinder was a critical component of the kit, especially in damp conditions, when it could not be gathered outdoors. Many materials make good tinder, including dry grass, cattails, or in this case, some flax tow from a frayed piece of rope.

Brimstone Matches

The predecessors to our modern matches could not be ignited by striking. They were slivers of wood dipped at both ends in molten brimstone (sulfur). When carefully applied to even very small embers, they produced a flame within seconds.

Striking Fire with Flint and Steel

Before the invention of the friction match, striking flint and steel was the best method for starting fires. The operation could be conducted in a matter of seconds and could be repeated many thousands of times with the same striker. The microcrystalline structure of flint is such that it is less brittle than other minerals of comparable hardness, yet it can easily be knapped into sharp shards. Other minerals, such as quartz or even granite, can be used in a pinch, though they are less effective.

1. A small piece of char cloth is held against the flint in the path of the sparks.

2. The steel striker is struck at a shallow angle against a sharp edge of the flint to project sparks onto the char cloth.

3. Where a spark makes good contact with the char cloth, it initiates a smoldering combustion in the form of an ember that grows rapidly.

4. The smoldering char cloth is wrapped in a bundle of fine tinder.

5. and 6. The char cloth is fanned by blowing until it is hot enough to ignite the tinder.

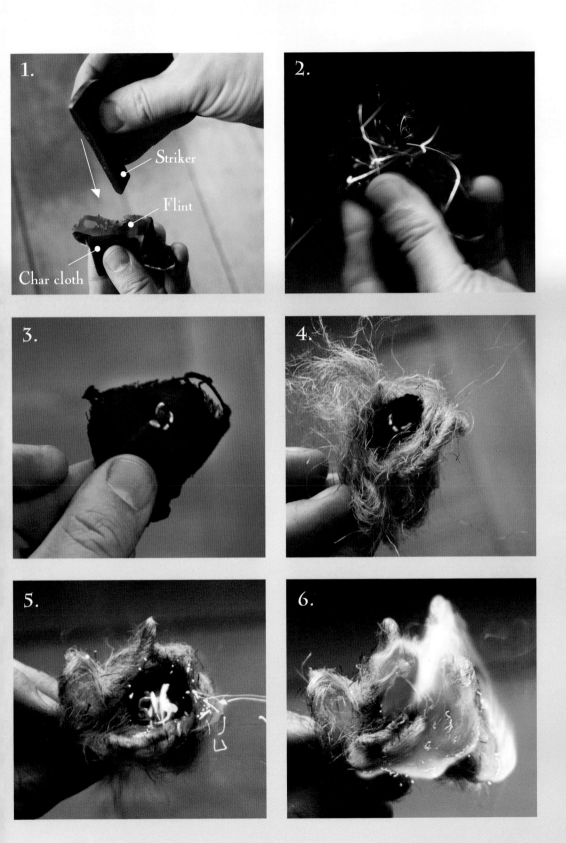

Playing Cards

Because of their popularity, playing cards were targeted by the British Stamp Act of 1765 that required tax stamps to be applied to items including newspapers and legal documents. This tax, widely perceived as unfair, inflamed American resentment to the cry of "taxation without representation."

Coins

Since British policies precluded the export of precious metal and coinage to the colonies, Americans adopted a complicated assortment of Spanish, French, and Dutch coins. The most common were the Spanish pistareens and pieces of eight. Away from urban centers, bartering and promissory notes were often preferred over currency transactions.

Continental Money

Lacking precious metal to strike coinage, the Continental Congress had no choice but to print paper money to finance the newly formed Continental Army. So much of the currency was issued to soldiers that it quickly lost value and was all but worthless by the end of the war.

Going to Boston

Popular dice games like "Going to Boston" or "Hazard" were the object of much gambling. Dice were easily carried anywhere and, if necessary, they could be improvised with a lead musket ball flattened on six sides as shown here.

Going to Boston Rules:

The first player rolls three dice and sets aside the dice (or one of the dice) with the highest number. The remaining two dice are rolled, and again, the die with the highest number is set aside. The remaining die is rolled one last time and the three dice are added up to determine the player's score. Each player takes a turn. The player with the highest score wins the round. At the end of a predetermined number of rounds, the player who has won the most rounds wins the game.

Smoking

Although it was already decried by some as a vile habit, tobacco smoking was well established in the colonies. Early in the 18th century, tobacco was smoked primarily in the evening at home or in taverns. By the time of the Revolution, more and more people carried tobacco pouches or boxes and indulged throughout the day. The tobacco box shown here features a burning lens in the lid, used to light tobacco by focusing the sun's rays.

Tobacco

In response to Europe's growing addiction, tobacco became one of the colonies' most valuable commodities. It is largely credited for financing the American war effort as collateral for French and Dutch loans.

Trump

The trump was a small musical instrument held against the teeth and plucked with the hand or finger. The trump was popular among soldiers because of its very small size and the fact that it required no formal training. One could easily produce enthralling rhythmic drones and even enough of a tune to support a little merriment around campfires.

British Regulars

British Regulars

British troops were superior to American militias in almost every respect. Their ranks were made up of career soldiers who were disciplined, fit, well trained, and well equipped. The American notion that British ranks were entirely constituted of criminals and riffraff was false. Although the majority enlisted as a means of escaping poverty, serving in His Majesty's army was a respectable profession. Since there was no shortage of volunteers early in the war, recruiting officers were discriminating, with a marked preference for young, healthy countrymen thought to present the ideal mix of vigor and respect for authority.

England took a scientific approach to warfare. Soldiers were subjected to deliberate and rigorous training programs remarkably similar to those of modern armies. Fresh recruits started with basic marching exercises, gradually working their way to weapons training and complex maneuvers. Some elite troops were even trained in swimming and climbing techniques.

Pay was very low, even by the day's standards, and all sorts of fees were withheld from the soldier's stipend to cover the cost of food, clothing, shoes, medical care, and other more or less dubious camp expenses. Discipline was extremely harsh. Even trivial offenses were swiftly met with lashings that were witnessed by the entire company. However, in spite of very demanding conditions, a good many soldiers managed to find some gratification in the service. Life in His Majesty's army was relatively comfortable and predictable, if somewhat regimented. The men took satisfaction in the camaraderie that inevitably formed, and they took pride in being part of the most formidable military force in the world.

The army was organized into regiments, each with distinct colors and traditions. Officers fostered pride in their regiment's legacy and encouraged a certain swagger to strengthen the soldiers' resolve in battle. The men were exhorted to live up to lists of honors and victories that often covered every continent. Each regiment was made of some combination of companies that could include infantrymen, light infantrymen, and grenadiers. Grenadiers were so named because their original function consisted in disrupting enemy formations with grenades, a role for which only the fittest and most daring men were selected. Although their role had changed, they remained an elite force that took pride in participating in the toughest missions. Light infantrymen were another group of elite soldiers selected for their mobility. While regular infantry constituted the relatively slow-moving core of a detachment, the light infantry was tasked with scouting, skirmishing, and rapid flanking maneuvers.

Drummers and fifers served crucial roles in every company. Various tunes signaled occasions, such as reveille, meal times, and musters. Under the tumult of combat, it was discovered that drumrolls and the high pitch of the fife were more discernible than officers' shouts. Therefore soldiers were trained to respond to a variety of musical cues. Men could be drilled and commanded almost entirely by the sound of the drum. Music and songs could also boost morale and quicken the step in long, strenuous marches.

Officers' commissions and promotions were usually purchased at substantial costs, thus limiting the status to the wealthy and well-connected. This corrupt system inevitably yielded a number of inept officers, but many were devoted and well schooled with a genuine passion for soldiering.

The British Soldier's Dress & Equipment

The red coats common to most British soldiers earned them the derogatory nickname "lobster backs." The color of the coat's facings and of hats, ornaments, and various details of the uniform varied from regiment to regiment at the discretion of the commanding officers and depending on the men's function.

The soldier on this page represents a light infantryman of the 4th Regiment of Foot circa 1774 as attested by the helmet, cartridge box badge, buttons, and various insignias.

1. Haversack
2. Bayonet scabbard
3. Wool breeches
4. Garter
5. Wool longstockings
6. Gaiter
7. Cartridge box
8. Second model Tower flintlock musket
9. Bayonet
10. Coat
11. Waistcoat
12. Leather helmet
13. Canteen

Epilogue

Following the skirmishes in Lexington and Concord in April 1775, the American War of Independence went on for eight years. Precise casualty tolls were not gathered, but an estimated 50,000 American soldiers died. More than two thirds of these losses were caused by disease or by mistreatment in British jails. On the British side, about 30,000 soldiers and 8,000 Hessian mercenar-

ies died. An unknown number of French, Spanish, and Dutch soldiers and Native Americans and civilians also lost their lives. At the start of the war, American rebels were no match for Britain's military forces, but in the course of the war, they managed to gain French, Spanish, and Dutch military and financial support. For the British, fighting a war more than 3,000 miles from home presented enormous communication and logistical challenges. Reports arriving in London and military orders sent back

to America were always several months out of date. Americans took advantage of a very large and familiar territory with prosperous farms and a strong tradition of local governance. British victories were always local at best and never significantly affected the American coalition as a whole. Furthermore, British military tradition was ill prepared for the type of skirmishing tactics that Americans had learned from a history of conflicts with Native Americans. Eventually, political support for the war waned in London as England was facing an escalating conflict with no clear prospect for victory. The surrender of General Cornwallis in Yorktown marked the final blow and prompted representatives to pursue a negotiated peace. The Treaty of Paris, signed on September 3, 1783, put an official end to the war. It was ratified by the United States Congress on January 14, 1784.

Index

A

Adams, Samuel 10
Alarm 8, 15
American War of Independence 9, 32, 60
Apostles 32
Arlington 11

B

Badger brush (shaving) 41
Bag 40. *See also* haversack, knapsack
Ball. *See* Lead ball
Ball puller 31
Bandolier 32
Barber 41
Barrel (gun part) 34, 35
Bartering 50
Bayonet 15, 18, 38, 58
Beans 43
Beaver felt hat 23
Beef 43
Birch bark 47
Birch tree 47
Blanket 40
Boston 7, 9, 10
Boston Massacre 8
Boston Tea Party 7
Bowl 42
Bread 43
Breech 35
Breeches 18, 22, 23, 58
Brick dust 30
Brimstone matches 47
British Regulars 56
Brookline 10
Brown Bess musket 27
Browning 30
Buckle shoe 25
Burning lens 52
Buttons 20, 26, 41, 58

C

Caliber 36
Cambridge 10
Candle 43
Canteen 18, 39, 58
Cap 23
Cartridge. *See* Paper cartridge
Cartridge box 18, 26, 28, 32, 34, 58
Casting ladle 36
Casualties 60
Cattails 47
Char cloth 47, 48
Charlestown 9, 10
Cider 43
Coat 18, 20, 58
Cock 27
Cockade 23
Cocked hat 23
Coins 50
Colonial Militia. *See* Militia
Colonies 6, 52
Concord 8, 10
Continental Army 18, 41, 50
Continental Congress 43
Continental money 50
Cornmeal 43
Cornwallis 61
Cotton 20
Cow 43
Cow horn 37
Cravat 20
Cup 42

D

Dawes, William 8, 10
Dice 51
Dice game 51
Discipline 57
Drill (military) 14, 57
Drum 57
Dysentery 41

E

Ember 47, 48
Enlistment 56
Etching 37
Eyeglasses 44

F

Farm 43
Fife 57
Fire 46, 47
Fish 43
Flash pan 26, 27, 34
Flax tow 31, 47
Flint 27, 28, 29, 46, 48
Flintknapping 29
Flintlock 18, 27, 34
Flintlock musket. *See* Musket
Flour 43
Fork 42
French and Indian War 6, 14, 27
Frizzen 27, 34
Frock 18

G

Gaiter 25, 58
Garter 24, 58
Going to Boston 51
Gourd 39
Grass 47
Grenadier 57
Gun flint. *See* Flint
Gunpowder 26, 29, 31, 32, 37

H

Half-cock 34
Hancock, John 10
Hard bread 43
Hartwell Tavern 9
Hat 18, 23
Haversack 40, 58

Heatstroke 39
Helmet 58
Hessian 60
Honey 39
Horn. *See* Cow horn
Hygiene 41

I

Ice 25
Ice creepers 25
Indian meal. *See* Cornmeal
Infantry 57
Ink 44
Ink stand 44
Insignia 58
Intolerable Acts 7

J

Jaws (flintlock part) 27

K

Knapsack 18, 40
Knife 42
Korean War 25

L

Lanolin 40
Lashings 57
Lead 29, 36
Lead ball 27, 28, 29, 31, 35, 36, 51
Leather 28, 29, 36, 39, 41, 58
Lexington 8, 9
Lexington and Concord 8, 60
Light infantry 57
Linen 20, 24
Literacy 45
"Lobster back" 7, 58
Longfellow, Henry Wadsworth 8
Longstockings 18, 24, 58

M

Massachusetts 7
Medford 10
Menotomy 11
Mercantilism 6
Mess kit 42
Militia 9, 10, 13, 14, 18, 27, 32, 36, 56
Militia muster 14
Milk 43
Minute Man National Historical Park 9
Minuteman 15
Molasses 43
Money 50
Music 52, 57
Musket 14, 15, 18, 30, 31, 34, 35, 36, 58
Musket ball 51. *See* Lead ball
Musket tool 31
Musket worm 31

N

Native Americans 14, 38, 60
Neck cloth. *See* Neckerchief
Neckerchief 20
Needle 41
Nightshirt 22

O

Officer 14, 23, 56, 58
Officers' commission 57

P

Paper 7, 29, 32, 35, 44
Paper cartridge 28, 29, 32, 34
"Paul Revere's Ride" 8
Pay 50, 57
Peas 43
Pelham, Henry 8

Penmanship 45
Percy, Brigadier General Hugh 9, 10
Pick and brush 26
Pieces of eight 50
Pistareen 50
Playing cards 7, 50
Pneumonia 41
Pork 43
Powder horn 18, 37
Precious metal 50
Prescott, Dr. Samuel 10
Priming charge 34
Puritanism 45
Pushpin 31

Q

Quill 44

R

Rain 25, 28
Ramrod 27, 35
Ration 40, 43
Razor 41
Reading 45
Redcoat 7
Regiment 57, 58
Reveille 57
Revere, Paul 8, 10
Ribbon 24
Rice 43
Rifle 14, 18, 27
Rope 47
Roxbury 10

S

Scabbard 18, 38, 58
Screwdriver 28, 31
Scrimshaw 37
Scurvy 39
Sewing kit 41
Shaving 41
Shirt 22
Shoe 25, 41

Shoe buckle 25
Skirmish 9, 30, 57, 60, 61
Slaves 6, 14
Sling 40
Smallpox 41
Smith, Colonel Francis 8, 10
Smock 18
Smoking 52
Smoothbore 27
Snow 25, 28
Soap 41, 43
Sons of Liberty 7
Spark 27, 46, 47
Spectacles 44
Spoon 42
Spruce beer 43
Stamp Act 7, 50
Steel striker 46, 48
Stipend 57
Straight last 25
Striking fire 48
Sugar 39
Sulfur 47
Switchel 39
Sword 18

T

Tallow 30, 46
Tavern 14, 52
Thread 41
Tin 39, 42
Tinder 48
Tinder box 46
Tinder fungus 47
Tobacco 52
Tobacco box 52
Tomahawk 18, 38
Touchhole 26, 27
Tower flintlock 27, 58
Townshend Act 7
Training 56
Treaty of Paris 61

Trump 52
Typhoid fever 41
Typhus 41

U

Underwear 22
Uniform 58

V

Vegetables 43
Vinegar 39
Vision impairment 44
Volley fire 14

W

Wadding 32
Waistcoat 18, 20, 22, 58
Water 39
Wax 46
Wool 24, 40, 58
Writing 44, 45

Y

Yorktown 61